Your Faith
HINDUISM

By *Harriet Brundle*

You can find the **bold** words in this book in the Glossary on page 24.

PHOTO CREDITS

CONTENTS

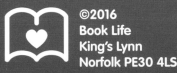

©2016
Book Life
King's Lynn
Norfolk PE30 4LS

ISBN: 978-1-910512-91-3

Written by:
Harriet Brundle

Designed by:
Ian McMullen

A catalogue record for this book
is available from the British Library.

What is RELIGION?

Religion means to believe in or **worship** something, usually a god or gods. Many religions have important places, celebrate **festivals** and help people to live a good life.

There are lots of different religions. The religions with the largest amount of followers are Christianity, Islam, Hinduism and Sikhism.

CHRISTIANITY

ISLAM

HINDUISM

SIKHISM

What is HINDUISM?

Hinduism is a religion that began over four thousand years ago. It is the oldest religion in the world and began in the country of India.

People who follow Hinduism are called Hindus. For Hindu people, their religion shows them how to live a good life.

BRAHMAN

Hindus believe there are many different Gods that all **represent** the most important Hindu God, called Brahman.

Hindus believe that Brahman is everywhere, all the time.

Brahman

Brahman is shown in three different forms. These forms are Brahman the **creator**, Vishnu the **preserver** and Shiva the **destroyer**.

Vishnu

Shiva

9

VEDAS

Vedas are a collection of four different books that are important for Hindu people.

Vedas are written in a special Hindu language called Sanskrit. Inside the different books there are poems, thoughts and ideas.

Children practise the reading of texts in Sanskrit at Jagadguru School.

PLACES *of* WORSHIP

Many Hindus pray at home. Hindus have a shrine, which is a special place in their house that has pictures of gods.

Hindu temples, called mandirs, are also places of worship. Hindus believe that the temple is a special place where they can feel close to their Gods.

MANDIR

Each mandir looks different to the next. Hindu temples were built to bring Hindu people together.

Hindus often bring fruits or flowers to the temple.
You must take your shoes off before going inside.

MARRIAGE

A Hindu wedding ceremony is called Vivaah Sanskar. For Hindus, marriage is very important because it is the start of a new family.

The wedding celebrations can last for many days.

The bride and groom take seven steps together and ask God for things such as food and children.

A Hindu wedding is very colourful!

KARMA

Hindu people believe that they live lots of different lives. Bad things that happen are because of things done in a past life.

This is called karma.

Hindus try to live a good life so that their next life will be better than the one before.

DIWALI

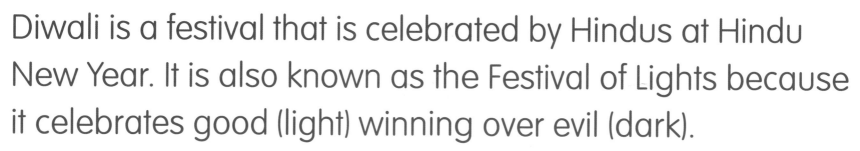

Diwali is a festival that is celebrated by Hindus at Hindu New Year. It is also known as the Festival of Lights because it celebrates good (light) winning over evil (dark).

Houses are filled with candles and many people go to watch firework shows. Friends and family celebrate by sharing gifts and food.

Facts about HINDUISM

1 Around 85% of all Hindus live in India.

2 Hindus respect the cow more than all other animals. They do not eat beef and **decorate** cows at festivals.

3 Hindus believe Vedas was written by gods.

4

Kashi Vishvamath Temple is one of the most special temples for Hindus. More than three thousand people visit it every day!

GLOSSARY

Creator someone who has made something

Decorate to add something, to make something else look better

Destroyer causing damage

Festivals when people come together to celebrate special events or times of the year

Preserver keeping something as it is

Represent to stand for or be a symbol of something

Worship to show a feeling of respect